Look Where He Brought Me From
A Spiritual Guide to A Transformed Life

By

Reverend Dr. Charles Darden

Copyright © 2024 by – Reverend Dr. Charles Darden – All Rights Reserved.

It is not legal to reproduce, duplicate, or transmit any part of this document in either electronic means or printed format. Recording of this publication is strictly prohibited.

Table of Contents

Dedication i
About the Author ii
Chapter One How It All Begins 1
Chapter Two The Enemy Thought He Had Me 4
Chapter Three Salvation: An Inside Job 9
Chapter Four Being Called Into The Ministry 14
Chapter Five Prayer Made a Difference 19
Chapter Six She Completes Me 24
Chapter Seven The Journey From Then To Now 28
Bonus: Chapter Seven The Journey From Then To Now ... 30

Dedication

I would like to acknowledge and dedicate this book to my deceased mother, Ruby Darden, and my grandmothers, Carlee Thurman and Emma Lee, who all prayed for me throughout my life's journey. During my sixty-three years, I've always been blessed by the Lord and recognized that I had a calling. After accepting Christ in 1982 and the call to minister in 1984, I knew my life was still incomplete.

Then I met the love of my life, Sadie Darden, a minister in the A.M.E Zion. We have been married for 39 years and have two daughters, Nicole and Genesis. They are both happily married to Jerrod Whistine and Chaddrick Doster. Sadie and I have four grandchildren, Jaidyn, Elijah, Chloe, and Jax, whom we love dearly.

We also have a God-daughter, Charita. She is married to Randy Williams. They have three children: Brennan, Cassien, and Sahana. I've been blessed by many who have poured into my life. I will mention them later in this book. Most of all, I thank my Lord and Savior, Jesus Christ, for saving me and giving me the determination to live in the Kingdom of God.

About the Author

Rev. Dr. Charles Darden is a 63 year old male, gospel preacher who grew up in a Christiana home. Born with pneumonia in both lungs, and was given a very little chance at life. However, his mother was a praying woman who believed in the power of prayer, she prayed for him and her prayers touched the heart of God. This has been a story and testimony he shares often with those he comes in contact with. He has been preaching in the A.M.E. Zion Church for 40 years and he has seen many people give their lives to Jesus Christ. In 1986 he married Sadie Hill and they became one. They have two daughters, Nicole and Genesis who have been wonderful girls. They both have two children who are a wonderful joy. He is a teacher, preacher, prayer warrior, and husband, father, and grandfather. His journey has been challenging, yet rewarding. To God be the Glory for the things he has done.

Chapter One
How It All Begins

Jeremiah 1:5 states: Before I formed thee in the belly, I knew thee; and before thou camest forth out the womb I sanctified thee, and ordained thee a prophet unto the nations. This passage has enlightened me to understand better the struggles, ups, downs, and mishaps I have experienced as a young man.

I was given very little chance of living due to having pneumonia, which almost robbed me of life at the time of birth. Most people realize that pneumonia is lung inflammation caused by a bacterial or viral infection in which the air sacs fill with pus and may become solid. Being premature, weighing only three pounds at birth, my mother was told to go home.

Doctors told her I wouldn't make it through the night. Understand here that God had a purpose for my life according to Jeremiah 29:11: "For I know the thought That I think toward you, saith the Lord, thoughts of peace, and not of evil, to give you an expected end."

My mother was a dedicated woman who believed in the power of prayer. She told the doctor, "Okay, you have done what you can, but I know another doctor."

My mother says she went home, dropped to her knees with tears in her eyes, and prayed as Hannah said, "Lord, I'm putting Charles Jr. in your hands."

Through prayer, God worked a miracle in my life. If you read this book and need a miracle, they still happen today. As I study the scriptures, I find at least three biblical tests for recognizing a legitimate miracle.

The miracle glorifies God. Miracles declare that God is active in our world and can disrupt nature's activities to reveal his character and accomplish his purposes.

The principle here is, "Does God receive the Glory?"

Beware of people such as Simon the Sorcerer in Acts 8:9 who boast of his greatness. Secondly, miracles stem from a righteous source. Jesus said that in the last days, false prophets will come and perform great songs and wonders to deceive, if possible, even the elect (Matthew 24:24).

Someone's words may sound true, and their actions may be impressive, but they are counterfeit if their lives show no good fruit. Thirdly, miracles ring true to the Holy Ghost. According to Paul, one of the gifts of the Holy Ghost is distinguishing between spirits (1 Corinthians 12:10).

Paul demonstrated this gift when he told Elymas, a Jewish sorcerer, that he was a child of the devil and an enemy of everything right (Acts 13:10). Through the Holy Spirit, Paul perceived that utter boldness that was in the man.

Likewise, we must look to the Holy Ghost for guidance regarding the source of a miracle. So, I say to all, believe in your miracle today. Another component that caught my attention and has impacted my life is the power of prayer displayed in my mother's and grandmother's lives.

Although I went to church with my mother and grandmother, their prayers helped me stay out of trouble growing up. Prayer has always fascinated me. The Bible talks a lot about prayer. This enriching subject can transform a person's life like mine.

Prayer is conversing with God; it's talking about life with the one who knows us the most. That's what my mother did. She spoke to God about her child struggling to live, and God heard her prayer and answered. I want to tell people reading this book today that God wants to change your situation through your prayer life. God is still working miracles; he is still healing bodies. He is still saving those who need to be saved—glory to God. A prayer is a powerful tool at a Christian's disposal. Jesus taught us to pray.

Matthew 6:9-13 says, "After this manner therefore pray ye: Our Father which art in heaven, Hallowed be thy name. Thy Kingdom come; Thy will be done on Earth like in heaven. Give us this day our daily bread. And forgive our debt as we forgive our debtors. And lead us not into temptation, but deliver us from evil: For thine is the Kingdom, the power, and the Glory, forever. Amen."

Therefore, prayer is a huge part of the Christian walk. Sometimes, prayer is private, and God calls us to close our doors and pray. (Matthew 6:5-8) This powerful prayer tool will have a lasting effect on your life and bring the miracle you need to experience.

Chapter Two
The Enemy Thought He Had Me

In this chapter, I want my readers to understand the real enemy. KJV dictionary definition of enemy is "A foe: an adversary." A private enemy who hates another wishes him injury or attempts to injure him to gratify his malice or will. The Bible makes it clear that we are fighting a spiritual, not physical, war against spiritual enemies.

"For we wrestle not against the flesh and blood, but against principalities, against powers, against the rulers of the darkness of this world, against spiritual wickedness in the high places." (Eph 6.12)

The evil we encounter in this world is due to Satan's direct influence and deception. Ephesians 6:11 warns us to " Put on the whole armor of God that ye may be able to stand against the devil's wiles." (KJV) As a churchgoer, I never really heard much about spiritual warfare and demons.

It wasn't talked about much in the Baptist tradition. Understand I am not trying to downplay the Baptist faith because I was taught many vital lessons by my mother and the church of choice she took us to as children. However, at the age of about 14, I was introduced to marijuana by those whom I began to hang out with. The enemy then deceived me into thinking I had to do what my friends did if I wanted to feel apart.

So, I found myself sneaking out the window at night just to hang out with my friends smoking marijuana and drinking alcohol. Often, when I said I wasn't going to do it anymore, I was threatened and bullied that they would jump on me, but I was afraid to tell my mom and dad. So, I left home at 15 to stay with a cousin, and this opened the door even wider for demons to enter.

I started not only smoking but also selling marijuana. It became a way for me to make extra cash. After talking to my mother, whom I respected, I thought entering the military would be a way to escape this kind of life. However, after entering the military, I became exposed to more drugs such as speed, yellow jackets, black Mollies, LSD, Sharm sticks, Acid, and cocaine.

The devil was trying to destroy my life. I started selling drugs at this point on the weekends. I was making seven to eight thousand dollars, living a fast life with women, and throwing parties. I was so deceived that church was nowhere on my mind until one night, as I was making a delivery, I saw blue lights behind me. I had been cornered by the cops while still in the military. My dad, at the time, was not living far from me in Texas.

He came to my rescue and said, "This is the first and last time that I am going to get you out of jail."

I got out, awaiting my court date. As the day approached, I was so afraid that I was going to spend time in prison for my possessions. I had a lot of marijuana when the Highway Patrol stopped me.

The judge looked at me and said, "Young man, I normally don't do this, but something is telling me you are going to make something out of yourself."

I was given six months' probation and had to report to an officer each week to see how I was doing. I had come to my wit's end with things like going to the clubs, drinking, and smoking became boring to me. I worked at a nursing home where I met this old saintly mother who began to talk to me about Jesus Christ.

I would enjoy her company. She couldn't see well, so she would want me to read the word of God to her. God was using this lady to draw me unto him.

Looking back, I can still see that feeble mother woods say, "Charles, you know Jesus can fix your life."

At this point, I decided to move from Texas to Mississippi, start all over with my life, and give God a chance. I started going to church with my grandmother. She was a missionary in the Church of God in Christ. My grandmother would often invite me to her house and pray over me.

She would say to me, "God has something special for you, Charles Jr."

I attended a service one Thursday evening where the power of God was so present that I experienced another miracle. God not only saved me but filled me with the spirit and delivered me completely from my drug addiction. I can't express my gratitude for that saintly woman in Texas and my grandmother. God had put me on the right path.

Although I was delivered from drug addiction, I need to mention here some of the biblical principles that I had to do to maintain my deliverance. Deliverance can be defined as being set free, having total freedom, or being made whole.

Through the Bible, we see Jesus healing many people and setting them free at different times, but we also see some who were healed and made whole, and that's what deliverance is. Deliverance is how

God shows mercy toward persons bound by various things and evil influences.

Furthermore, deliverance is an expression of God's conventual mercy and compassion. When Jesus came, he came to bring judgment, but he also came to bring mercy, salvation, deliverance, and healing, which are all manifestations of God's mercy. Deliverance and healing are based on the mercy of God, God's loving-kindness, and God's Conventional loyalty. When we look at Jesus' ministry, we see him:

- Healing the sick
- Casting out devils
- Raising the dead
- Cleaning the Leapers
- Opening Blind eyes
- Unstopping deaf ears
- Losing dumb tongues

All these are forms of how he delivered people from the situations they found themselves in. I have always been fascinated with the ministry of Jesus Christ. Jesus Christ's ministry, as I understand it, was built on three pillars according to Kimberly Daniel's book "Clean House."

Life, Labor, and Love are the categories that he put forth to minister to individuals. St John 10:10 says, "Jesus came so that we could have abundant life."

He died a harsh death so that we could have life and have it more abundantly. Matt 26:38 says, "Jesus labored in the Garden of Gethsemane until the job was finished. He labored unto death. St John 11:35-36"

When Jesus ministered to the crowds, He was moved with compassion. Jesus wept when Lazarus died, and the people witnessed how much he loved him.

These three attributes make up the ministry of Jesus Christ. Scripture tells us that there is life in the blood (Genesis 9:14). For us to live and have freedom, Jesus had to die. John 15:13 says Greater love has no one than this than to lay down one's life for his friends.

So, know that God's power is always available for you and me. You can be delivered in whatever area of life you struggle physically and spiritually. In the words of the late Bishop Patterson, "Be healed, Be Set free, and Be delivered in Jesus' name."

Chapter Three
Salvation: An Inside Job

I want to dispel some things here in this chapter. Because of my upbringing, I often thought salvation was different until I had a "Born-Again" experience myself that changed my whole life around. Growing up, I thought I was all right because I had been baptized early.

Furthermore, I was a good old guy who didn't bother anybody and didn't cuss until you made me mad. I joined the church and sang in the choir. However, I lived a sinful life on the weekends. None of those things I mentioned will save a person. Salvation is solely by "grace through faith" (Eph 2:8).

This scripture passage is the heart and soul of the gospel message seen through Scripture. Here, I need to discuss that we need to have the right understanding of grace and faith. God's grace does not change a person's standing before God, yet leaves his character untouched. Real Grace is not a license to do whatever we choose.

According to Scripture, true grace teaches us "To deny ungodliness and worldly desires and to live sensibly, righteously, and Godly in the present age" (Titus 2:12).

Grace is the power of God to fulfill our new covenant duties. I don't want to over-emphasize Grace without mentioning Faith in the process of salvation. Saving faith is inseparable from repentance, surrender, and a supernatural longing to obey.

Repentance is always at the core of genuine saving faith. Repentance involves a recognition of one's utter sinfulness and a turning from self and sin to God (1 Thes 1:9)

Repentance is not a human work; it is the inevitable result of God's work in the human heart. So, I must say that those who are truly born of God have a faith that cannot fail to overcome the world (1 John 5:4).

Understand even when you give your life to Christ, you and I will sin (1 John 2:1) we will sin, but the process of sanctification can never stall completely. God is working on you even as you are reading this book. I would like to look at Paul's emphasis on salvation.

Romans 10: 1-17 says Brethren, my heart's desire and prayer to God for Israel is that they might be saved. For I tell them that they have a zeal of God, but not according to knowledge. For they, being ignorant of God's righteousness and going about to establish their righteousness, have not submitted themselves unto the righteousness of God.

Christ is the end of the law for righteousness to everyone who believes, for Moses describes the righteousness of the law that the man that doth these things shall live by them. But the righteousness of faith speaketh on this wise, say not in thine heart who shall ascend into heaven (that is to bring Christ down from above) or descend into the deep (that is to bring Christ again from the dead) but what saith it.

The word is nigh thee even in thy mouth, and in thy heart: That is, the word of faith, which we preach; that if thou shalt confess with thy mouth the Lord Jesus and shalt believe in thine heart that God hath raised him from the dead, thou shalt be saved. For with the heart man believeth unto righteousness and with the mouth confession is made unto salvation. For the scripture saith whosoever believeth on him shall not be ashamed.

For there is no difference between the Jew and the crook; for the same Lord over all is rich unto all that call upon him. For whosoever shall call upon the name of the Lord shall be saved.

How then shall they call on him in whom they have not heard? And how shall they hear without a preacher? And how shall they preach except they are sent? As it is written, how beautiful are the feet of them that preach the gospel of peace and bring glad tidings of good things! But they have not all obeyed the gospel for Esaias saith Lord who hath believeth our report. So then faith cometh by hearing and hearing by the word of God.

In Romans Chapter 10, Paul set out to expound the doctrine of salvation clearly and simply. Here in Romans, it seems that Paul is trying to clarify the way of Salvation to new believers in Rome.

Growing up, I heard all kinds of doctrines on what it meant to be saved; however, I understand the true way of salvation can only come through the name of Jesus Christ.

Acts 4:12 says, "Neither is there salvation in any other: for there is none other name under heaven given among man, whereby we must be saved."

In this text, Peter explains to the Sanhedrin whose authority he used to heal a lone man (Acts 3: 1-10). Specifically, the council asks, by what power or name did you do this? (Acts 4:7) Peter claims that he did it through the name of Jesus Christ of Nazareth (Acts 4:10). Understand that one's name includes the sense of one's identity, power, authority, and reputation. Jesus' name is the only name that saves.

"Salvation" is from the Greek root word saved. It means deliverance and preservation and can imply rescue in a worldly, physical context, such as from enemies, or it can suggest eternal spiritual rescue. The salvation that Christ offers delivers us from sin, and hell preserves us or keeps us safe for heaven.

St John 10:28 reminds us of these very important feet when it says, "And I give unto them eternal life, and they shall never perish, neither shall any man pluck them out of my hand."

Salvation, furthermore, can be explained as the fact that since God has wrath for sin, no one can be saved apart from God's help. I think about my own life before Christ. I tried worldly living, drugs, dancing, clubbing, drinking, and other things.

None of these things brought peace or assurance in my life. When I met Jesus Christ, things began to change. This change helped me to understand the process of salvation. By sending his one and only son to die for our sins, God made a way not just for me but for all who will come to Christ. See what God did here: input our sin upon Christ, who paid the penalty and input as his righteousness by faith.

Furthermore, there is truly no other way to be saved since we are born in Adam, in sin, and all die. Our sinful nature is inherited since the fall, and we sin because of sinfulness. Our salvation cleanses us from sin by only one name, Jesus Christ. Since we must have an ultimate sacrifice, only the Son of God, who is the only one born sinless, can save us.

All persons must understand that our salvation is a heavenly gift from our Father. Understand it is a complete work of grace and mercy. We must be saved by this name alone and the gift of life promised to those who believe in the name of Jesus Christ. Salvation was never meant to be complicated, as Dr. Otis McMillian has often said in his book "The Roman Road to Recovery."

He says some preachers are complicated, confused, and even distorted the message of salvation to the point that man wonders. Does anyone know? Is anyone sure what to believe? There are so many denominations. Can they all be right? The confusion of our day is nothing new.

If salvation was and is a God thing, God's word is the best source for the truth about this subject. I pray that you, as a reader, embrace biblical teachings in the word of God that will give you a perfect picture of salvation according to the riches of the word of God. Salvation is an inside job that only God can perform.

Chapter Four
Being Called Into The Ministry

Ministry is an awesome commission from God to lead his people as an undershepherd or spiritual leader. Isaiah 32:7: "How beautiful upon the mountains are the feet of him that bringeth good tidings, that publiseth peace; that bringeth good tidings of good, that publiseth salvation; that saith unto Zion, Thy God reigneth! I accepted my call in March 1984 at my mother's church in Jackson, Mississippi.

I was so excited and had a heart to see people saved, healed, and delivered. The scriptures give us an indication of what it means to be called into ministry. In Matthew 4:18, some of the disciples are summoned by Jesus while doing something else. Paul's dramatic experience is described in Acts 9.

Although many of us don't have dramatic experiences, certain incidents help influence one's calling. In my case, my mother and Grandmother positively influenced my life as they demonstrated love, prayer, and Christian service. My Godly mother believed in Sunday School and worshiped as two pillars to help her children live productive lives.

On the other hand, my grandmother put a lot of emphasis on Praise, Fasting, and Deliverance. God used both my mother and Grandmother to direct me into ministry. If the truth be told, I struggled with my call for some months before I realized that if I was going to move forward, I needed to do what God wanted me to do. Amid the struggle, one thing that came to my mind was how people would perceive me, knowing I was a past drug addict.

The enemy tried to fill my mind with doubt about how God could be calling me to do ministry, and I used to do drugs. As I continued in bible study and personal study of the word of God, I realized that 2 Cor. 5:17 says, "Therefore if any man is in Christ, he is a new creature old things passed away; behold all things become new."

Therefore, I had to come to grips with the enemy's strategy to keep me from doing what God wanted me to do. My Pastor then, Dr. Jessie Redmond, is instrumental in guiding me through my ministry calling. I met with him weekly as he mentored me, and I would always travel with him to conventions and other preaching engagements that he had. He was a great sought-after preacher all over Mississippi.

God gave me a great foundation through this saint of a pastor, where I began to develop my ministry. I would often go out weekly and bring others who didn't have a personal relationship with Christ to church.

My Pastor would just smile and say to me, "God is using you to do Evangelism," which I didn't know much about at the time meant to be an evangelist.

All I knew was I had a burden to see people saved, delivered, and set free like I had experienced. At the time of my calling, I had no college education, but my Pastor pressed upon me about the importance of preparation as a part of the ministry process.

The famous Baptist Preacher Gardner C. Taylor once said, "The one who lacks preparation does not have a grasp of such issues as where the gospel comes from, how it grows up, how to grow out, and what effect it has had on people throughout history."

Preparation was always a strong point of my Pastor's ministry, so he, along with the church at the time, Cherry Grove M.B. church, sent me to a two-year school at Natchez Jr College, where I enjoyed the rich experience of private seating that helped me to understand and appreciated what my home church had invested in me as a young preacher.

I understood that Theological training was crucial to my preparation for ministry. I didn't want to get caught up in just obtaining knowledge but wanted to know where God was leading me and how having a good Theological education would help me get there. As I know it, theological study seeks to interpret and understand revelation.

I strongly believe in theological education; I have often thought it is the best way to prepare those who have received the call to minister. Ministry itself involves preparation, even more preparation, and also involves more than preaching. It includes seeking a relationship with God about whom the word has dealt and the Christ toward whom it points.

In other words, one is not called just to preach the word but to preach what the word seeks to say. The calling into ministry is a serious matter that all people need to take solemnly because we are dealing with souls in the Kingdom of God.

Preparation is important not only to the ministry but also to a minister's character. I have seen so many preachers who had the gift of preaching but had no character, which can distort the Gospel message they attempt to preach.

One author has said, "A sermon lived is remembered more than he or she attempts to preach."

Another author said, "A sermon lived is remembered more than a sermon preached. Or I'd rather see a sermon than hear one any day."

There is a lot of truth in these statements because often, as humans, it's hard for people to understand the flaws of a person who has been called that they, too, have faults and failures. Although I mentioned this, the standard for all who have been called is to live a holy and consecrated life before God. They should walk in integrity where people will be more prone to listen and follow the way of Christ as they see him operating in our lives.

O Clay Maxwell Sr, a longtime pastor of Harlem's Mt Olive Baptist church, says, "It is a very pitiful gospel we have if it does not exceed who we are."

The worth of our ministry is found in God. As the Jewish scholar Abraham Heschel said, "The gospel is a story of God in search of humanity."

Furthermore, the preacher must depend on the power of the Holy Spirit in ministry. Ray S. Anderson mentions and raises the importance of the Holy Spirit as it relates to doing ministry in his book "The Soul of Ministry." I'm convinced that whatever area of ministry one is called to do, one needs to be empowered by the Holy Spirit if we are going to be effective.

We can learn from the Early Church in the book of Acts, where we see the manifestation of the Holy Spirit operating in ministry. In "The Misunderstanding of the church," Emil Brunner says that the key to the success of the first-century church is not historical memory but the fellowship of the spirit.

He further says, "The spirit operates with overwhelming revolutionary, transforming results. It manifests itself in such a way as to leave one wondering why and how and in such a way as to demolish the walls of partition separating individuals from each other. People draw near the Christian community because its supernatural power irresistibly attracts them."

As men and women of God, we must never forget who we represent as we travel this road called ministry. I have had a wonderful ministry journey, Pastoring for 32 years in the AME Zion church. I have traveled to many places spreading the Gospel of Jesus Christ, and for that, I'm thankful.

Chapter Five
Prayer Made a Difference

My adventure in learning to pray began when I was young. I listened to my mother and grandmother pray, which has impacted my life and ministry. My mother was my teacher and a model of a praying Christian.

On the other hand, my grandmother was more vocal about her prayer life; she often talked about fasting and praying, which intrigued me. Both of these women had busy lives, but one thing they did was model prayer, which has been with me my entire life. I want to start by saying I've read many books about prayer, but Paul Cedar's book "A Life of Prayer" has given me the purpose of prayer.

In this chapter, one must understand the purpose of prayer if we will be effective in our prayer life. Author Phillip Brooks wrote," The purpose of prayer is not to get man's will done in heaven but to get God's will done on Earth."

This statement serves as my foundation for how vital prayer is to all aspects of the Christian journey. Prayer has helped me walk in obedience and commune with God and taught me how to align my agenda with God's. The Bible is filled with God's instructions for his people to pray.

Sometimes, he invites us to come to him in prayer. Other times, he firmly commands us to pray. Look at some of the invitations from God as he invites man to communicate with him.

"Seek the Lord while he may be found; call on him while he is near." (Isa 55:6), "Ask, and it will be given to you" (Matt 7:7). "Pray continually" (I Thess 5:17). "Then Jesus told his disciples a parable to show them that they should always pray." (Luke 18:1) Prayer for me is essential to the Christian life if one is going to be victorious and effective in ministry.

The Theologian Martin Luther said well: To be Christian without prayer is no more possible than to be alive without breathing.

The challenge I have experienced in ministry for both clergy and lay is that we often allow the business and demand of ministry to consume us and often don't prioritize prayer. Our Lord has invited all of us and commanded us to pray.

Let me pause here and say that if you take time and develop a prayer life, your life and ministry will be more enriching as you travel on your Christian journey. As a believer, I want to share some principles about prayer that I have developed on my journey in ministry.

First, I had to view my daily prayer time as a relationship with God and not some legalistic duty. When we look at Scripture, it's important to note that the Pharisees spent much time in regular prayer and fasting, yet they had no personal relationship with God. A powerful prayer life is not just a discipline or ritual.

I believe it is your commitment to a personal relationship with God. Prayer must be viewed as your commitment to spend meaningful time in a personal relationship with God.

John 17:3 says, "And this is life eternal, that they might know thee, the only true God, and Jesus Christ whom thou hast sent."

How do you think it makes God feel when we make little or no time to be alone with him as believers and people of God? In a busy society, we must relearn the crucial lesson in Luke 10:38-43. In this biblical narrative, Mary and Martha were sisters with different views of what mattered to God. Martha was busy doing all kinds of tasks for Jesus but had no time to just fellowship with him.

On the other hand, Mary prioritized sitting quietly in his presence and listening. Tragically, most believers are more like Martha than prayerful Mary. We are so busy with God that we spend very little time with him. Our priority should be to spend time with the Lord. In John 15:5, Jesus clearly states that we can do nothing unless we maintain a close relationship with him.

We can only maintain such a relationship by spending time in regular prayer. The second principle I want to mention is that we must consistently commit to spending time alone with God in uninterrupted prayer. Matthew 6:6 says, "But when you pray enter into your closet and when you have shut the door, pray to your father which is in secret shall reward you openly."

Therefore, it is crucial that, as believers in the Lord Jesus Christ, we spend time with God consistently. As we view the prayer practices of Jesus and New Testament believers, it is clear they regularly spend much time alone in fervent prayer. If Jesus and the early church spent much time in prayer, what about you and me? God's requirements have not changed.

Unfortunately, what has changed is many people's definition of what constitutes a powerful prayer life. Beyond question, developing a compelling prayer life requires consistent time alone with God. Paul said in Thess 5:17 prayer without ceasing.

In Luke 11:1, Jesus' disciples made their wisest request when they said, "Lord, teach us to pray."

This is perhaps the greatest request any Christian can make of the Father. We only learn to pray by praying. This lesson has caused me, as a preacher and believer, to rely on prayer when I couldn't rely on anything else.

When I lived in Knoxville, Tennessee, my baby girl was pregnant with our granddaughter Chloe. I received a call from my wife that I needed to get there because she was having some complications. Before leaving and getting on the road, I paused and talked with God.

When I arrived at the hospital, many family members were gathered. They all had a strange look on their faces. I thought for a moment, *What's going on?*

My wife approached me and explained to me what was going on. She said with a trembling voice my daughter almost went into cardiac arrest and that they couldn't find a heartbeat for my grandbaby. I kept praying as I entered the room and held my daughter's hand. I prayed with her and assured her that God had everything under control.

The truth was the baby had turned green with no life, but prayer was made for her, and she came back to life. Chloe is now nine years old. She is a beautiful young lady who is determined to reach her goals and enjoy the beauty in life. This is a testimony of what prayer can do in a believer's life if they pray consistently.

Thirdly, a powerful prayer life must be biblically balanced. It's almost like a diet. In a balanced diet, we regularly eat from all the primary food groups and in proper amounts. We all know what happens if you only eat from one or two food groups and completely ignore the others. We would become sick from malnutrition.

The same principle applies to a balanced prayer life. In general, there are five basic types of prayers. If you only pray one or two types of prayers regularly and neglect the other three, you and I will not have a powerful growing relationship with Christ.

To be weak and inconsistent in any one of the basic prayer types is to be weak in our relationship and service to God. As you seek to develop a healthy relationship with God, this particular prayer will aid in that process.

1. Praise, Thanksgiving, and Worship

2. Confession and repentance

3. Petition and supplication

4. Intercession

Meditation (listening, prayer, and reflection)

Chapter Six
She Completes Me

Reflecting on the 36 years my queen and I have been married, I am eternally grateful for this journey. Christian marriage involves a great act of faith if one takes marriage promises seriously. Marriage has taught and compelled me to be less selfish and more concerned about my mate.

To live up to the impossible promise of Christian marriage, "For better or for worse," requires God's help.

Marriage, for me, is about respecting and honoring each other. Much of that comes from both parties involved in having a personal relationship with God. I met my wife at Alcorn State University in Lorman, Mississippi, while attending Natchez Jr. College. I was involved with the president of the college, who had a stroke and needed assistance in his home.

I went to help daily as a caretaker. Several women were there during that time, but Sadie caught my attention. She was somewhat shy, and I was too. I started by studying the Bible with her. Then, I had a preaching engagement and asked her to join me. She did with a smile.

After several months of dating and getting to know each other, I asked her to marry me. I drove her home to her aunt, who was living with her at the time, and asked to marry her daughter. She consented and told my wife I now believe you have met the right one. We were married in December of 1986.

It was beautiful, and we will always cherish it. I must say to everyone reading this book that marriage is like your relationship with the Lord. You must constantly work on it and talk to each other. Looking back, I had to deal with my trust issues. Past relationships with others can hinder your present relationship with your spouse if you don't heal from the old baggage.

Other relationships had hurt me. My wife had hurt from the past as well. We had to grow and learn to trust each other. I told her we are here to stay for a lifelong journey, so we must discuss what bothers us. I must mention that I was private when talking about what was happening to me.

I would often say, "I was alright," and all the time, my wife knew when something was bothering me.

Communication between you and your spouse is important in the relationship. Good communication will bring peace and harmony. Bad communication can trigger discord and suspicions. Good communication can facilitate healing. Bad communication can cause pain and sickness. Good communication can produce and enhance love.

Bad communication can spread bitterness and hostility. I am married to the sweetest woman I have ever known. She completes me with her presence. She respects me for what I stand for and who I represent. She told me before I married her that she would never get in the way of my ministry and God.

She has kept her word. Reflecting on our growth through marriage and our relationship, I have learned much about using words. Words spoken at the wrong time can cause damage. God had to work on me and my wife in this area because we are both strong-willed and needed to humble ourselves to God first and then to each other.

I remember creation and how powerful words are. When God created the world, God spoke it into existence: Genesis 1.3. says, "God said Let there be light: and there was light."

In regards to marriage, a lot of things are spoken into existence. Think about it: if we say," I don't trust you enough, the reality is created. We can hurt or punish our spouse with words. We can make our spouse sick or destroy them with words. So, I tell all couples to be careful about what we put into words.

However, there is some good news: words can help bring healing and a sense of building up each other. Words of encouragement, appreciation, kindness, and love can work incredible miracles in your marriage. I am a witness to that.

Choosing my words has brought healing to my own life. I have also seen God transform my wife's life by learning to humble myself and use words that build her up rather than tear her down. Building a successful and lasting relationship in marriage is demanding and complex.

No simple slogans will suffice. What works for one couple may not work for another. My wife is outgoing, and it irritates her to stay in the same setting without venturing out, going to other towns, and traveling to see different parts of the country. Some are okay with being right where they are, so you must know what works in your relationship.

My wife and I took our wedding vows seriously. Especially when it says "loving and honoring each other." Both love and honor are action verbs requiring much more than lip service. Honoring is an old-fashioned term suggesting respect and promoting expressions of recognition.

It may mean telling your mate "Thank you" for the little things one takes for granted, like preparing meals, cleaning the house, or taking the garbage. Long-lasting martial relationships require discovering and living with the acts of compromise and forgiveness. Our interests are different, so we must learn to compromise.

My spouse and I have learned to do things that each other enjoys. This has strengthened our relationship and brought so much happiness to our marriage. Through all of the joys and challenges of our marriage, Psalms 121:1-2 has helped us remain faithful to God and each other. It says, "I will lift up mine eyes unto the hills, from whence cometh my help. My help cometh from the Lord, which made heaven and Earth."

Chapter Seven
The Journey From Then To Now

My journey started when I accepted my calling to ministry in 1984 and preached my first sermon. A few years after accepting my calling to ministry, I met the love of my life, Sadie Darden. When we met, she was a God-fearing young lady with great aspirations.

We started out studying the word together, and it all came together in 1986 when I asked her to marry me. We were both in college and didn't have many resources at that time, but we always worked together. I was in school, and she was too. After getting married, we settled in Nashville, Tennessee, and our first daughter was born.

Nicole is a beautiful young lady who is full of life. She has grown up to become a productive young lady with two kids. We also have a second daughter named Genesis. She is married with two children. Genesis is doing well in her life. In 2000, God blessed us with a bonus daughter, Charita.

We have poured into her life from then till now. Charita is a very smart young lady who we have watched grow spiritually and mature. She is married with three children. They have been a big part of our lives. Charita has had many hardships in her life, one being the loss of her mother.

As Godparents, we have been there to give her spiritual and moral support. My wife and I have tried to set a good example through our ministry before our children as well as our congregations. From my first pastoral assignment until now, I have always had strong and vibrant relationships with my youth and children.

This is an area where ministry has always been a concern. Scripture teaches us to train them up in the way they should go. I believe part of that training is being a good example before them that will last.

My pastoral ministry has been in the AME Zion church from Mississippi to Arkansas, Tennessee, South Carolina, North Carolina, and back again where my children are. I took a detour in 2009 to leave South Carolina to care for my father, who died from cancer in 2012.

Since then, I have had a burning desire to become a chaplain and care for the needs of those suffering with life issues. In 2024, I am enrolling in a chaplain program at Hood Theological Seminary, where I plan to start working toward my goal.

I have pastored and served fourteen churches since 1988. I have enjoyed the pastoral ministry, where I have preached, administered, baptized, buried the dead, and given pastoral care. To God be all the Glory for the things he has done.

Bonus:
Chapter Seven
The Journey From Then To Now

It all came together in 1986 when Sadie and I got married. We were both in college and didn't have a lot of resources at the time, but we always worked together.

During a conversation, Sadie said, "Being a family in the ministry is like a mirror. As a minister's wife, you have to watch over all aspects of your family. The upkeep of the family is important. Sometimes, things weren't easy, but prayer has helped keep our peace and strengthen us."

She says, "My husband can handle anything that comes his way. Overall, it has been a joy and a learning Christian experience. God has been good to us in the midst of it all."

After getting married, Sadie and I moved to Nashville, Tennessee, where our first daughter, Nicole, was born. She is a beautiful young lady and full of life. Nicole is now married with two children. Nicole says, "I remember my dad getting up to speak.

I admired my father's ability to love everyone and treat people respectfully even if it wasn't given back to him." It wasn't easy being a preacher's kid. It was hard to build friendships, but on the other hand, we were able to gain exposure to different cultures. She knew essentially the things she did were a reflection of him, making her rebellious.

Nicole says, "I didn't want to fit into a mold, but God has covered me. It has helped me to be in the place I am now."

We have a second daughter named Genesis. She is also married with two children. Genesis is very smart and beautiful. Genesis said she was glad she was able to meet people and travel.

"Getting food first was a good thing." Genesis laughs.

Even though the journey has had many challenges, Genesis says, "My father is optimistic. He wants to see the good in people."

The most amazing part was having a spiritual leader in the same household. She was able to witness the lifestyle of a Christian and Christian marriage.

In 2000, God blessed us with a bonus daughter, Charita. We have been able to pour into her life from that time until now. She is a very smart young lady who we have seen grow spiritually and mature with her family. Charita is married with three children.

During her journey, she has had many hardships, one being losing her mother. My wife and I have been there to guide and support her.

Charita says, "I am thankful for the love and support my God's parents have given me. They have shown me strength, courage, and hope. I admire their daughters, who genuinely treat me like a sister. They have been with me every step of the way, the good and the bad. My Godparents have provided an example of a good and faithful Christian life. They are evidence that prayer and following God's word works."

Through our ministry, we emphasize family and try to set a good example before our children as the congregations we pastor. From my first pastoral assignment until now, I have always had strong and vibrant relationships with my youth and children.

This is an area where ministry has always been a concern because Scripture teaches us to train them how they should go. I believe part of that training is being a positive example before them and building a lasting relationship with them.

All of my pastoral ministry has been in the AME Zion church. From Mississippi to Arkansas, Tennessee, South Carolina, North Carolina, and back again. I wanted to be in South Carolina, where my children are, but in 2009, I decided to leave South Carolina. I left to care for my father, who died in 2012 from cancer.

Since then, I have had the burning desire to become a chaplain who cares for those suffering from life issues. In 2024, I am enrolling in the chaplain program at Hood Theological Seminary. There, I plan to start working toward becoming a certified chaplain.

Throughout my ministry, I have pastored and served fourteen churches since 1988. I have given pastoral care to many congregations. I have administered, preached, baptized, and buried the dead in the ministry. I give God all the Glory for all the things he has done.

www.ingramcontent.com/pod-product-compliance
Lightning Source LLC
Chambersburg PA
CBHW040025130526
44591CB00027B/8